WWI The Sorrows of Victory

About the Author

Born in Udaipur, Rajasthan the mesmerizing city of lakes, I, Dia Bagla am 17 and currently a student at The International School Bangalore (TISB).

As I dwelled more into studying The World War and history, from just a subject it became my inspiration. What puzzled and amazed me the most were the feelings of patriotism these soldiers had in their hearts, the burning desire, the courage, and the strength with which they fought. Knowing their death was evident yet they stood strong with their heads high, facing the attack at all times; a big salute to them.

Also, what led me to write this book was the way that events that might seem so avoidable are capable of triggering such a colossal global conflict.

The truth is, no matter how much ever we may hate wars but they have somehow shaped our today and that is undeniable. Wars leave an important and relevant mark on our lives and this has driven me to bring together 'The Sorrows of Victory'.

I wanted our young readers to understand & visualize WW1 in the simplest and most chronological manner so that they can value their today.

WWI The Sorrows of Victory

Dia Bagla

Published by Zorba Books, March 2023
Website: www.zorbabooks.com
Email: info@zorbabooks.com
Author Name : DIA BAGLA

Title: WWI The Sorrows of Victory

Printbook ISBN: 978-93-95217-64-4
Ebook ISBN: 978-93-95217-65-1

Zorba Books Pvt. Ltd. (opc)
Sushant Arcade,
Next to Courtyard Marriot,
Sushant Lok 1, Gurgaon – 122009, India

Printed by Manipal Technologies Limited
A1 & A2 Shivalli Industrial Area Manipal Udupi, Karnataka – 576104

Table of Content

Acknowledgments

I would like to acknowledge the tremendous thanks I owe to my parents, who have been my biggest inspiration to strive hard to achieve my goals and be the best version of myself.

I can only credit my ardent passion for history to my high school history teacher, Mrs. Riji Anil Kumar at TISB, who ignited this passion with the way she taught, making history more than just a subject to me.

I would also like to thank Sneha Bawari for her immense help and guidance in editing this book, without which it would not be what it is now.

All information in this book is from extensive research done by me from various history books and the substantial knowledge found on the internet through different sites.

Chapter 01

The Beginning

A load of bravery in their guts
A raging desire to defeat their enemies
A feeling of patriotism in their hearts
A foreboding instinct that there might be no tomorrow
And yet a smile on their faces to bid farewell to their families.........

War was never as gruesome, heart-wrenching, and globally dominating before the dawn of World War 1. This war redefined the very idea of power, hostility, and destruction, embroiling countries in its trap like never before. World War I, 28th July 1914 - 11th November 1918.

World War I, also called the Great War, was one of the most brutal, fearsome, and harrowing conflicts of all time. *4 years 3 months, and 2 weeks* of misery, anxiety, and dilemma; taking the lives of nearly more than 9 million soldiers; 21 million and more wounded, and more than 10 million civilian causalities.

A global conflict between more than 30 nations entrapped in a web of slaughter, carnage, and destruction. A period of passion, greed & envy like never before yet the feelings of patriotism, sorrow & defeat prevailed, definitely one of the deadliest & darkest wars of that time.

It embroiled most of the nations of Europe along with Russia, the United States, the Middle East, and other regions. The war pitted the Central Powers: mainly Germany, Austria-Hungary, and Turkey—against the Allies: mainly France, Great Britain, Russia, Italy, Japan, and, from 1917, the United States.

Try imagining the brutality, the blood-shed, the agony!

Have you ever tried to picture how the war really was and why even this war? What were the reasons, the causes, and the motives behind this whirlpool of blood, hatred & envy?

Was it simply the kind of fight in Avengers where they fight over infinity stones (for all you Marvel fanatics!) or do you think countries just fought because of some personal grudge between the rulers or was it much more?

The outbreak of this multifaceted war was a consequence of not one but many underlying factors prevalent at that time. In order to understand these and hence the situation of Europe (where the war originated from), here is an easy to learn acronym: 'M.A.I.N'.

M.A.I.N:

- **Militarism:- Militarism was the fierce competition between countries to build forces and arms.** *If your friends own something that you don't, don't you go and ask your parents to buy it for you too?* Countries followed the same logic when it came to guns, forces, and infantry.
- **Alliances: - Countries throughout Europe made deals with each other to defend themselves against potential rival countries.** *For example - Russia and France were on the same side during this period of World War 1 while Germany and Austria-Hungary were in an alliance. Even before WW1 started* the following countries were in an alliance:
    - Russia and Serbia
    - Germany and Austria-Hungary
    - France and Russia
    - Britain and France and Belgium
    - Japan and Britain
- **Imperialism:- when a country increases its power and wealth by bringing additional territories under its control.** European countries had many ways of trying to be more superior and powerful. One of these included conquering smaller countries which they called 'colonies'. The more colonies they ruled, the more domineering they perceived themselves as. As countries saw their fellow countries acquire more colonies, they joined this manic rat race too.
- **Nationalism: - Nationalism, as we all know is the feeling of intense patriotism and loyalty towards one's country.** For the rulers and people of these countries, just building military forces, alliances, and acquiring colonies weren't enough, they also wanted to prove the superiority of their country and their devotion towards it. In order to achieve this, they often resorted to ways of aggression and force.

Now imagine the strained atmosphere in the continent of Europe where all its countries, with their various alliances, were so divided and with each under the grips of feelings of desire and over competitiveness.

Chapter 02

The Trigger

M.A.I.N – As discussed in the previous chapter, these factors formed the backbone of the cause behind the ebullition of this war but what exactly transformed the situation in Europe from one of hostility to one of war?

The era of 1914 dates back to the time when countries were ruled by kings and queens.

Today, the rule in our countries lies in the hands of a democracy, which simply means "Of the people, by the people, and for the people," as quoted by Abraham Lincoln.

However, in the 1900s, one ***monarch ruled the entire nation*** which gave him/her all the power in the country, making him/her the most influential person.

Having said that, the main trigger that catalysed this war was the **assassination of the heir to the throne of Austria-Hungary at that time,** Archduke ***Franz Ferdinand.***

An illustration showing the assassination of Archduke Franz Ferdinand and his wife Duchess Sophie.

Source - https://www.newspapers.com/topics/world-war1/assassination-of-archduke-franz-ferdinand/

How & why?

Serbia and Austria-Hungary, both European countries, wanted to conquer a small country called Bosnia-Herzegovina. (Connect this back to one of the M.A.I.N factors – imperialism)

Austria-Hungary simply wanted Bosnia- Herzegovina due to their desire of expanding their empire but Serbia wanted to annex it for a different reason.

Slavs was the name given to a group of people who were the common population of Bosnia-Herzegovina and Serbia. *You would always want to stick to your group of friends right?* Similarly, Serbia wanted all Slavs to be under it's control.

Source - https://www.bbc.co.uk/teach/does-the-peace-that-ended-ww1-haunt-us-today/zf4cscw

This map shows Serbia, Bosnia-Herzegovina (as marked by Bosnia on the map), and the empire of Austria-Hungary or the Austro-Hungarian Empire.

Finally, it was Austria-Hungary who ended up capturing Bosnia-Herzegovina, this obviously didn't go well with Serbia.

When powerful countries like Austria-Hungary conquered smaller ones like Bosnia-Herzegovina, they often positioned troops there to maintain control.

Archduke Franz Ferdinand and his pregnant wife Duchess Sophie went to the capital of Bosnia-Herzegovina (Sarajevo) on 28th June to check on military troops that were positioned there.

Serbian terrorists were enraged, as they couldn't capture Bosnia-Herzegovina and hence dropped a bomb on the carriage that the heir and the duchess were traveling in. However, luck stood by them and they escaped death. But as it's often said, good things don't last forever.

Later that day, a 19-year-old Serbian nationalist, *Gavrilo Princip,* shot them, resulting in their ultimate death

He belonged to a Serbian terrorist group called the Black Hand.

July Crisis (1914)

This assassination gave rise to the July Crisis of 1914 which was a period of turmoil and unrest. During this period, Austria-Hungary (who wanted to get back at Serbia) sought assistance from its only major supporter, Germany.

Germany pledged to fully stand by Austria-Hungary. This was mainly because- firstly, their alliance with Austria-Hungary, secondly, Germany thought that by reacting to this assassination, it would assert its influence and dominance. Thirdly, they thought that Serbia's major supporter, Russia, would not be prepared to involve itself in a war to defend Serbia. Lastly, Germany also thought a war against Serbia would be an easy win for them which would increase their influence in Europe.

Hence, Germany gave Austria-Hungary what is called a *'blank cheque'*, as a token of promise of full-fledged support. All these events took place in the first week of July.

However, Austria-Hungary was still wary about declaring war on Serbia because of the other European countries, their possible reaction to this and also, they did not want to be portrayed as an aggressive country jumping to the option of war. Hence, they started drafting an ultimatum (a demand, which if not met, would cause consequences) to be given to Serbia.

This ultimatum included some terms and requirements as follows-

- Serbia had to prevent the spread of negative information against Austria-Hungary or its emperor
- It had to disband all nationalist organizations (like the Black Hand)
- It had to allow representatives from Austria-Hungary to enter Serbia and investigate the murder of Archduke Franz Ferdinand and remove and arrest people from the Serbian government that they found to be guilty and involved in actions against Austria-Hungary

This ultimatum was given to Serbia on July 23rd.

This period became known as the July Crisis.

Serbia's reaction to this ultimatum was one of agitation and anger.

fun fact

One of the alliances in Europe before World War I was called the 'Triple Entente'. The member countries of this particular alliance were Britain, France, and Russia. These countries were in full agreement of the fact that the terms of this ultimatum were pretty harsh. Eventually, these countries actually ended up fighting the war on Serbia's side!

When they did not accept this, a furious Austria-Hungary declared war on Serbia on 28th July.

With the prevalence of the M.A.I.N factors along with this assassination, war was imminent.

Let's have a quick overview of what we've explored so far:

1. ***What were the four main causes of World War I?***

If the mnemonic M.A.I.N is the first thing that comes to your mind, you're absolutely right! Militarism, Alliances, Imperialism and Nationalism are the 4 main causes of World War I but not the immediate cause. So, there's your next question.

2. ***What was the immediate cause that actually triggered World War I?***

Maybe the name hasn't really settled in your brains quite yet but yes, it is the homicide of the heir to the throne of Austria-Hungary. Archduke Franz Ferdinand! (But make sure to remember that he wasn't the only person killed, his wife Duchess Sophie who was pregnant was also shot along with him).

Archduke Franz Ferdinand

3. ***Which rival country shot Archduke Franz Ferdinand with his wife?***

a) France

b) Russia

c) Serbia

d) U.S.A

If you're thinking 'c', your answer is correct! It was Serbia.

Gravilo Princip, the assassin

Chapter 03

A Division of Power

The magnitude of this war itself tells us that the war was just not confined to one or two countries, rather it had engulfed all of Europe, forming groups and alliances.

So, which countries were involved in this World War, and how exactly were they divided?

But before we move on to the alliances formed during this war, let's take a look at the alliances that existed even before the onset of this war.

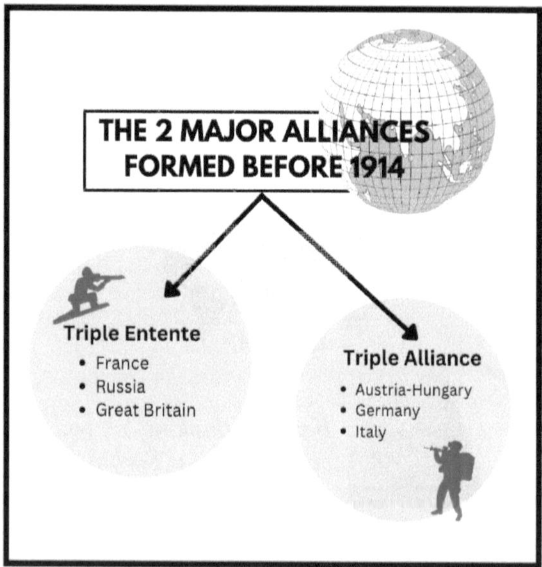

Moving onto the alliances formed during WWI:

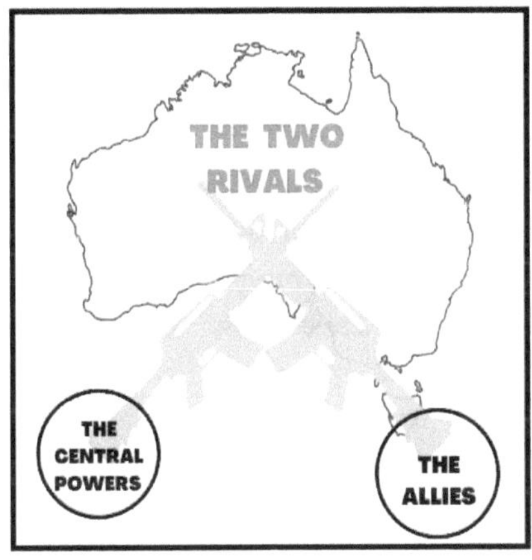

THE ALLIES / THE CENTRAL POWERS

THE ALLIES	THE CENTRAL POWERS
• Belgium • Britain • France • Greece • Italy • Japan • Luxembourg • Portugal • Romania • Russia • Serbia	• Austria-Hungary • Bulgaria • Germany • Turkey

This table will help you distinguish between these two sides in a more systemized manner.

As you can see, the whole of Europe got divided into 2 main big groups- The Central Powers and The Allies and each of the countries supported one group depending on their relations and strength.

NOTE - *Many of these countries mentioned above had empires and several colonies. Empire simply means an extensive group of states and countries ruled by a Single monarch, and colonies, as mentioned earlier, is a country or an area under the full or partial control of another country and ruled and controlled by settlers of the ruling country. For example, the empire Austria-Hungary had, was often referred to as the Austro-Hungarian Empire or the Dual Monarchy.*

Source - https://aboutartnouveau.wordpress.com/2012/11/28/ vinkovci-croatia/austro-hungaria-1914/

Can you see the region outlined in red on the map? That was approximately the Austro-Hungarian Empire. Huge, right?

If you come across the term 'Ottoman Empire', don't let it baffle you.
Ottoman Empire was also known as the Turkish Empire because it was ruled by the Turks. The country of Turkey was developed after the end of World War I but for the sake of simplicity and understanding, Turkey has been used sometimes in place of the Ottoman Empire. But it is important to note and remember that Ottoman Empire consisted of various other regions as well. This Empire ceased to exist after World War 1 and was completely broken down.

Similarly, Russia, Germany, Britain, France, and the Ottoman Empire were also empires. This meant that numerous countries were under their rule.

Sadly, this meant that many of these smaller countries also found themselves at war when the countries who controlled these empires joined the forces. For example, Australia, Canada, India, and New Zealand being a part of the British Empire, were dragged into the war as soon as Britain joined.

But now I am sure you must be intrigued to know how these countries even divided and joined either The Allies or The Central Powers.

It is important to note that this wasn't an overnight process but a bond or understanding or grudge of years that moulded these rivalrous alliances. The process by which these countries aligned themselves in these alliances, marking the progress of the war, is commonly known as the **DOMINO EFFECT.**

Chapter 04

The Domino Effect

Domino Effect was basically the influence of a country on the other which led them to join the war. Each country's entry into the war brought another country along with it because of their alliances, pacts, or simply their agreements to defend each other when in need. This was like a chain of countries joining either side one after the other, which is how this became a global war and spread to various parts of the world.

Each domino contributed to the progress of the war which made it so colossal.

This was literally like a game of tug of war where each side struggled to attain a more powerful team in order to witness the fall of the other one.

As said earlier, many countries got involved in the war because of their prior alliances.

You might think it was silly of them to jeopardize the safety of their own country just to protect another country but this tells us the significance and strength of the allies formed earlier.

In order to be secure, they had to risk something.I guess you can't have all you want without giving in to something!!

So, the rivals and groups were formed in the name of protection, benefits, or simply a powerful empire acquiring a lesser powerful country. But how exactly did this partnership between countries affect the war and lead to the domino effect?

I am sure we all at some point have played a game of dominos, where if placed accurately, when you knock the first domino, it causes a chain reaction and causes the rest to fall. This type of chain reaction is exactly what we will be seeing in this chapter.

Let's get started on the various dominos that constituted this domino effect. Imagine each of these events as one domino each:

The very **first domino** which stimulated Austria- Hungary to declare war on Serbia was, you guessed right, the **homicide of Archduke Franz Ferdinand (heir to the Austria-Hungary throne).**

After Austria-Hungary in cooperation with Germany declared war on Serbia, Russia also began to prepare its army to defend Serbia. *This was because these two countries were intimately related as they shared a common population of Slavic people.*

Heard this name before? Yes, these Slavs also lived in Bosnia-Herzegovina and Serbia. But remember, Serbia and Russia were not actually bound by a formal alliance but this common population of Slavs played a big role in uniting them. Further, Russia internally always thought of itself as The Great Power and dreamt of conquering Austria-Hungary and Germany.

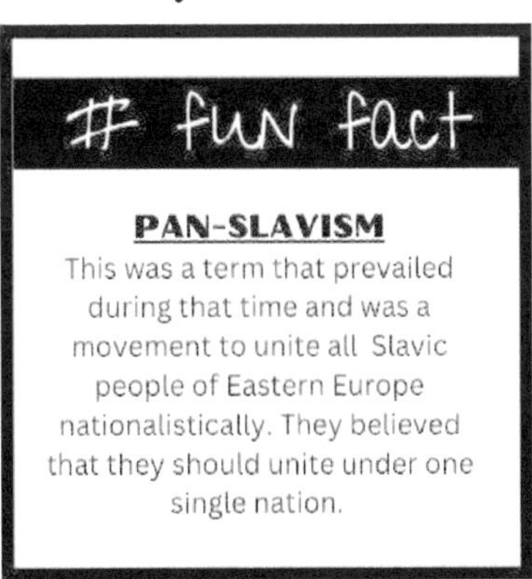

The **second domino** was when Germany, which was in alliance with Austria-Hungary, trailed on to offer its most valuable support and hence entered World War I, forming a part of The Central Powers by declaring war against Russia *(the supporter of Serbia)*. As France and Russia were in an alliance at that time, when Russia joined the war, France also got dragged in and started preparing its army.

Now, Germany decided to wage war against France, and simultaneously, it also invaded Luxembourg. **This was the next domino.**

Why Luxembourg?

- Firstly, Germans believed Luxembourg to be a German state and wanted full control over it.
- Secondly, its proximity to France was a key factor as it would help them to set up a military base that would immensely help in the battle with France.

Next to join the war were Belgium and Britain. Germany decided to attack France at its weakest frontier, which at that time was Belgium where the military was least trained. Britain who had earlier promised to protect Belgium from any kind of attack got involved in this war due to the German attack. Another selfish or you can say – self-protective reason for Britain's involvement was because Belgium's ports lay in close vicinity to the British coast.

 # fun fact

The German leader Wilhelm Kaiser said that Britain had joined the war over a "scrap of paper" (a reference to Belgium!). Well, he clearly wasn't content about Britain's involvement in the war against his own country!

If the Germans took over Belgium, it would be detrimental to Britain too as sooner or later they could eventually get captured.

Britain's entry into the war bought Japan into it as well because of their prior alliance.

Who Would Have THUNK It?

A secret treaty was signed between Turkey and Germany which stated that after Germany waged war on Russia, Turkey would enter the war on the side of the Central Powers. However, this treaty was not officially signed by all members of the Turkish government and hence did not work out as planned. As Turkey delayed joining the war, Germany offered it a gift of two ships and a huge loan. This gave way to Turkey's entry into the war.

Then, Turkey joined Germany. This was mainly for two reasons: First, there was a secret treaty between the two, formed in August 1914, and second, Germany offered a gift of 2 warships and a huge loan to Turkey.

Italy also joined The Allies when they persuaded it with the promise of land.

This would have given you an idea of how the domino effect worked. Ironically, enticing countries with land (greed for expansion) became a common way of expanding their allies.

Bulgaria joined The Central Powers (Austria-Hungary and Germany) in 1915 by declaring war on Serbia because of the lure of territorial expansion.

Source - https://www.mpsaz.org/fremont/staff/dlseeley/elp/versailles/participants/maps_europ

When the war started, Romania which was to the south of Bulgaria (as you can see on the map) and shared common borders with the same, chose to remain neutral because while its king Caro II wanted to side with Germany, the political heads were in favour of The Allies. However, the king died in October 1914 and was replaced by King Ferdinand I who wanted to support The Allies.

An ironic observation is that both Romania's king's and the deceased Austria-Hungarian heir's names were Ferdinand!

Romania also had some selfish interest to join the Serbians as they wanted to seize some territory from Hungary which was home to many Romanians.

On the other hand, The Allies (the group of countries supporting Serbia) wanted Romania's support because it could cut off rail communications between Germany and Turkey and also Germany's oil supplies. Britain to lure Romanians on their side even made some loan offerings to Romania while France organized a military training mission and Russia made a promise of modern ammunition. The Allies also promised that they would send at least 200,000 soldiers to help Romania launch an invasion into Austria-Hungary to protect Romania from Bulgaria.

The Romanians, however, only joined the war in 1916 when The Allies sent a note stating that they could either join the war on their side now or never. Under this pressure, Romania joined The Allies in August 1916 with a declaration of war on Austria-Hungary.

Can you begin to imagine the intensity and the need for both sides— The Central Powers and The Allies to strengthen their empires to win the war?

Additionally, because Portugal and Britain were in a former alliance, Portugal helped Britain in 1916 by capturing some German ships. This led to the Germans declaring war on Portugal in March 1916 and hence, Portugal joined the war too.

Greece wanted to maintain neutrality when the war broke out because although Greece and Serbia were in an alliance, the king of Serbia was married to the German emperor's sister and did not want to support The Allies. However, a government that supported The Allies had been formed in Greece in 1916, and in 1917, the Allied

Powers blockaded Greece, landed their troops in a Greek city, and demanded that the king abdicates. The next day, the king was forced to abdicate due to these factors and Greece joined the war in favour of The Allies.

I hope by now you can visualize and understand how the domino effect came into play. Here's a flowchart to help you memorize the Domino Effect better!

The assassination of Austria-Hungary's heir, Archduke Franz Ferdinand by a Serbian terrorist.

Austria-Hungary so livid at this homicide that it declares war on Serbia.

Russia (Serbia's old ally) mobilizes its army to defend Serbia.

Germany (Austria-Hungary's ally) declares war on Russia in support of Austria-Hungary.

Since France and Russia were in an alliance, Germany waged war on France simultaneously.

Germany attacked Luxembourg which was next to France. This was because it was an ideal location for the Germans to base their military.

Invading France required a well-designed and strategic plan, which is why Germany attacked it at its weakest frontier:- Belgium. This marked Belgium's entry into the war.

Britain had promised to protect Belgium against any attack which is why Britain joined the war against Germany.

↓

Britain's ally Japan joined the war on its side.

↓

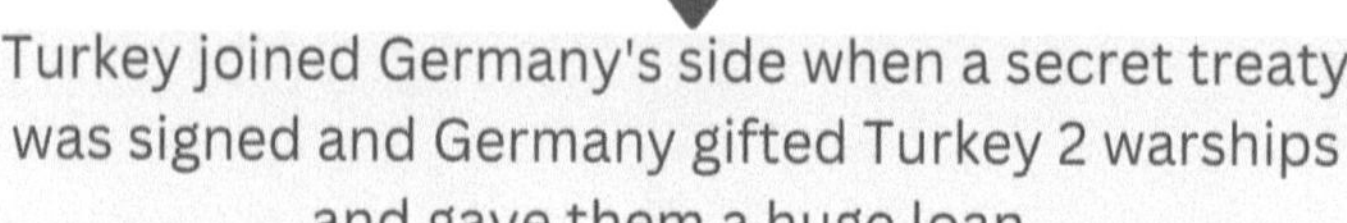

Turkey joined Germany's side when a secret treaty was signed and Germany gifted Turkey 2 warships and gave them a huge loan.

↓

Italy, who was earlier a part of the Triple Alliance with Germany and Austria-Hungary turned its back on them when it was offered land and territory by The Allies.

↓

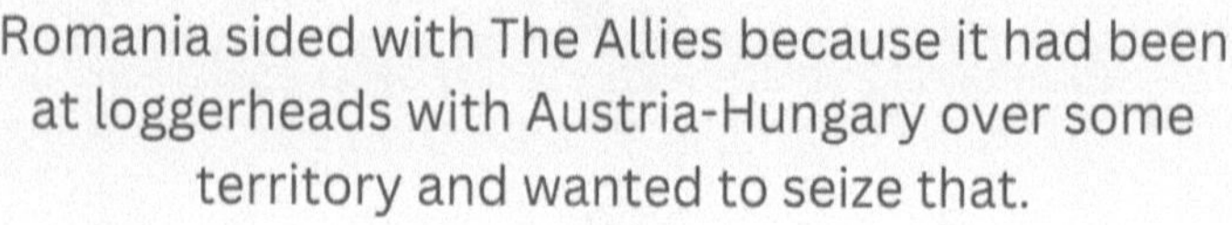

Romania sided with The Allies because it had been at loggerheads with Austria-Hungary over some territory and wanted to seize that.

↓

Bulgaria joined the war on the side of The Central Powers because it desired some territory it thought it would gain if it won the war on The Central Powers' side.

Source- https://slideplayer.com/slide/17660918/

CLARIFICATION CENTRE

If you're wondering why Germany seems to be taking all the action even though it was Austria-Hungary's battle to fight, your doubt is 100% valid!

On July 5, 1914, Germany handed Austria-Hungary something called a "blank cheque". Through this, Germany gave Austria-Hungary its word of honor that it would wholeheartedly support Austria-Hungary in any of Austria-Hungary's endeavors against Serbia. It is believed that this was one of the deadliest mistakes committed by Germany. When Austria-Hungary turned to Germany for its solemn promise of undeterred assistance, Germany gave this check because it thought that not reacting to Archduke Franz Ferdinand's death would undermine its influence in Europe and also because it did not expect Russia to be prepared for war. This "blank check" is also known as the "carte blanche".

I am sure the question lingering inside your head right now is the absence of the mention of the US. Undoubtedly, it has always been considered a strong and powerful country.

It was involved in this war but why has it not been mentioned up till now?

This is because USA wanted to maintain neutrality since many people in the US saw the war as a dispute between powers that had nothing to do with them. Also, there were many immigrants living in the country which led to split opinions on the war. USA's president, Woodrow Wilson, believed in the policy of neutrality and announced in 1914 that his country would be *"impartial in thought as well as in action"*.

It did indeed join the war (on The Allies side) but towards the end in 1917, the reason for which you will learn later in the book. Its entry in the last and most excruciating time of the war immensely helped The Allies.

Other countries that joined the war in 1917 were China and Thailand. These countries joined the side that they thought was most likely to win in order to receive a share of the fruits of victory. If I gave away the side these countries joined right now, it would soak out all the fun so hold onto your guesses for the end!

Chapter 05

The Schlieffen Plan

If you go back to the previous chapter and the domino effect, you will notice that Germany waged war on Russia and France at the same time. **Was this a smart move?**

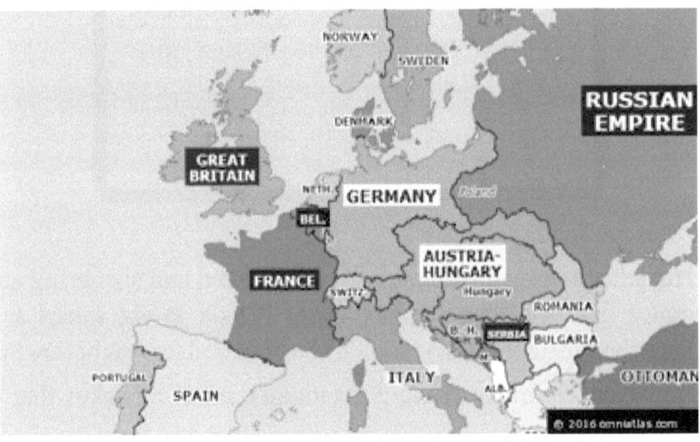

Source- https://omniatlas.com/maps/europe/19140804/

Look at this map of Europe from 1914.

France and Russia are on opposite sides of Germany. So, now Germany had embroiled itself into a conundrum—- how could it fight two enemies at once? To do so, it would have to divide its forces, which means that it would fight both France and Russia with only half of its capability. Germany could not afford this as this practically spelled failure.

Hence, they employed a plan called the "Schlieffen Plan".

This plan was drafted by ***General Count Alfred Von Schlieffen***, the German officer after whom it was named. This plan worked out how the Germans would defeat both France and Russia but not simultaneously as to avoid splitting their forces in half and mitigating the power of their invasion.

Who Would Have THUNK It?

The Schlieffen Plan (implemented in 1914) was actually devised by General Count Alfred Von Schlieffen in December 1905. He came up with this plan because of the high anticipation of an impending battle. This was because by 1905, France and Russia were already in an alliance against Germany. Further, Europe had been divided into 2 alliances, namely The Triple Entente and The Triple Alliance. This plan was further revised and enhanced in 1914.

What was the Schlieffen Plan?

This plan involved launching an unexpected and shattering attack on France first and then moving on to Russia in six weeks as the Germans thought that Russia wouldn't be prepared for war before that.

However, Germany made 3 seemingly small mistakes that cost them a **big loss:**

- Germany underestimated Russia when it thought it wouldn't be ready for war before six weeks.
- It undermined France's military capacity when they presumed that conquering it in 6 weeks would be an easy win for them.
- The Germans prophesied that this plan would work for them perfectly and hence didn't care to draft any backup plans.

Nonetheless, the Germans did not understand the defects of this plan at that time. So first let's understand how the Germans executed this plan which will make the shortcomings of this plan clearer.

How did Germany invade France?

Belgium was located right next to the weakest point on France's border (as marked with red on the map) and the Germans wanted to exploit this.

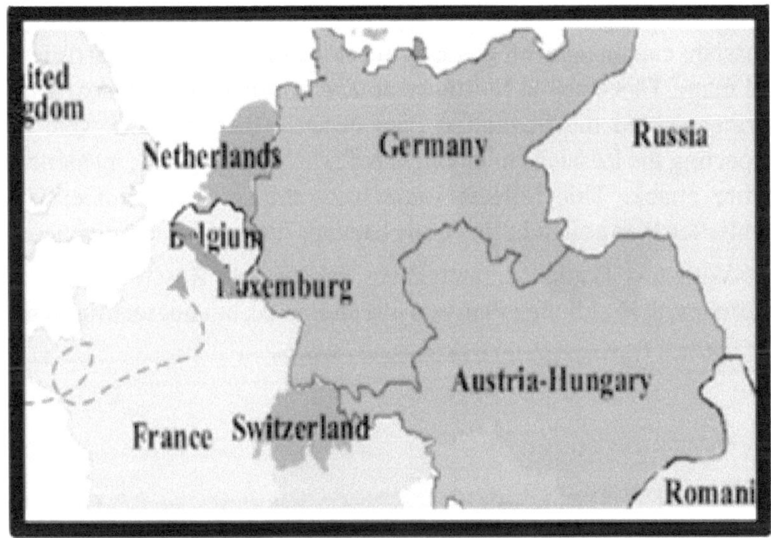

THE RED ARROW POINTS TO THE WEAKEST BORDER

Source - https://www.nationalarchives.gov.uk/pathways/firstworldwar/maps/europe1914.htm

Germany invaded Belgium on 2nd August. This also marked Britain's entry into the war as Britain had promised to protect Belgium from any conflicts. However, this was also because Britain did not want Germany to win the war and have complete control of Europe.

The inception of Britain in this war is rather ironic as the Germans expected the least resilience from Belgium but this cost them another rival, and a powerful one, Britain.

It's intriguing to see how quickly the tables turned on the Germans, who thought their plan was foolproof.

Britain and Belgium had signed a treaty way earlier in 1839 where Britain promised to shield Belgium against any invasion. Now implementing its deed, Britain declared war on Germany on 4th August for charges against Belgium.

Hence, Britain entered the War on the side of The Allies.

Britain sent its armed forces called the *British Expeditionary* Force (abbreviated to BEF) to strengthen the defence. provided by Belgium. These two forces combined succeeded in decelerating the German army's speed, serving as an impediment to their plan.

While the Germans were busy attacking France and Belgium, the Russians caught them off guard by attacking them from the east (refer to the map). This came to be known as *The Battle of Tannenberg,* which further dented the Schlieffen Plan because the Germans were not expecting the Russians to mobilize before 6 weeks, let alone an entire attack. This reflects some hazy thinking in the Germans' Schlieffen Plan as it didn't have any backups for the slightest diversion.

With this Battle of Tannenberg, which was Russia's attack on Germany, the Schlieffen Plan was just hampered, but **not terminated**.

We will read further about it in the next chapter.

Chapter 06

The Battle of Tannenberg & The First Battle of Marne

Source - https://www.wikiwand.com/en/Battle_of_Tannenberg

A picture of a burning Gasthaus on 27th August (during The Battle of Tannenberg). A Gasthaus is a small inn or hotel in a German speaking country or region.

BATTLE OF TANNENBERG (1914)

This was a battle initiated by Russia on Germany and lasted from 26th August to 30th August 1914. The Russian Generals planned on invading Germany from 2 different sides, the southwest and the northeast to lessen the chances of a powerful retaliation from the Germans.

However, poor communication between the two Russian armies invading from different sides curbed a well-planned and effective attack. Worsening the situation for Russia, the Germans intercepted a few of the Russian messages which gave them the upper hand as they cut off all Russian supplies. **This battle was a victory for the Germans and it furbished them with ammunition they captured from the Russians.**

A Picture of Russian prisoners captured

Source - https://www.britannica.com/event/Battle-of- Tannenberg-World-War-I-1914#/media/1/582679/232325.

Progress of the "Schlieffen Plan"-

By the time the Germans entered France and were well placed to launch an attack on its capital, Paris, Britain, and France organized their troops along the River Marne where they ambushed the Germans. The Schlieffen Plan required the Germans to move swiftly with high speed, inevitably making them victims of severe fatigue. Their army split due to this extreme tiredness, which is exactly what The Allies capitalized on in a battle called the Battle of Marne.

THE FIRST BATTLE OF MARNE (1914)

Named after River Marne in France, this was fought between the Germans on one side and the French army along with the British army called the British Expeditionary Force (BEF) on the other side.

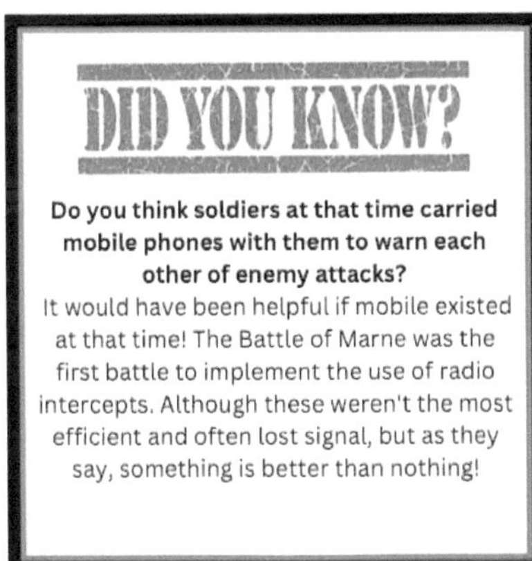

This battle took place from 6th September to 12th September 1914. The Allies took advantage of how exhausted the German soldiers were at that time because the Schlieffen Plan which they had been following required high speed and exertion for their attacks.

The Battle of Marne was considered a huge success for the allies as they prevented the Germans from conquering France or Russia even though they lost a large number of soldiers in this aggressive war.

During this battle, the French used reconnaissance or spy planes to be able to attack better.

A picture of German soldiers during this battle, wearing the Pickelhaube helmets

Who Would Have THUNK It?

If I ask you what vehicles you think were used in this fierce Battle of Marne, you would probably say fighter planes or military vehicles. A taxi is understandably the furthest thing from your mind, right?

Yes, those taxis that we use to go to a friend's house or the market. In France, they were used to get troops on the battlefield. These taxis were known as 'Taxis of the Marne'.

The 'Taxis of the Marne'

Source - https://www.sortiraparis.com/arts-culture/histoire- patrimoine/articles /259038-history-fact-it-happened-on-september-7-in-paris-paris-taxis-requisitioned-the-taxis-de-la-marne/lang/en

Chapter 07

"Necessity is the mother of invention": Trench Warfare

As we know by now, for The Central Powers things weren't exactly going as they had perceived. Schlieffen Plan wasn't in any way successful and The Battle of Marne acted more like a nail in the coffin. They had lost a lot of the army, the soldiers were wounded, so many of them had died and the remaining were exhausted and losing faith.

Like nowadays, communication and commuting weren't exactly simple and easy at that time. Further, they didn't have helicopters or planes to carry the deceased or wounded soldiers, or even supplies.

Then how did the Germans protect their lives and the lives of their fellow soldiers after they failed in The Battle of Marne?

Definitely, the soldiers couldn't travel all the way back to Germany as they literally had no means to do so. As they say, *'Necessity is the mother of Invention'.*

These soldiers started digging tunnels underground, called ***trenches,*** during this war. These trenches acted as temporary hiding spots where soldiers spent days living, attacking, and taking shelter.

The Germans started digging in order to avoid losing any more ground during this battle of Marne, obviously, they didn't want to retreat as that would mean failure and would also give the opposing side more area to capture.

Eventually, as more and more soldiers belonging to both sides started using the trenches as a way to hide and gain shelter, fighting inside these became unavoidable.

This form of war was called Trench Warfare, translating into war in the trenches or tunnels.

This Trench Warfare took place throughout the war on the Western Front.

Interesting, isn't it?

TRENCH WARFARE

This warfare seemed effective as it not only hampered movement or advancement but also prevented either side from being able to gain a lot of land on the western front. By the end of 1914, trenches built by both sides stretched from the North Sea and throughout the areas of Belgium and France to Switzerland.

Look at this map and locate the North Sea, France, Belgium and Switzerland. This area was essentially the western front of the war

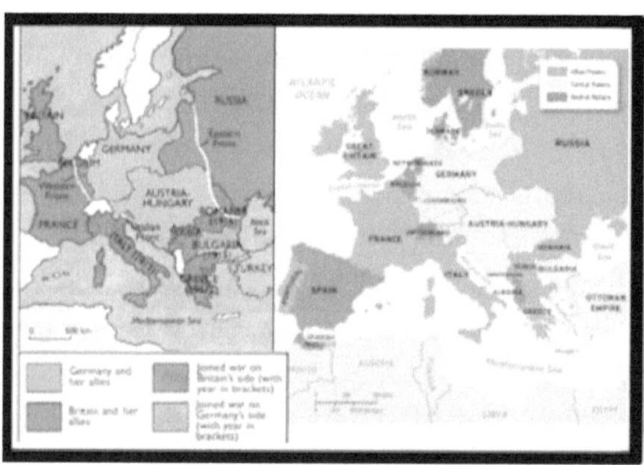

Source - https://spartacus-educational.com/FWWtriple.htm
Source - https://history.delaware.gov/world-war-i/

Through this form of warfare, both the rivals wanted to outmaneuver the other, in the process building trenches that would go around the other one's side. This way they could gain the upper hand by attacking in a way that completely ambushes their rival.

However, these armies used spotter planes to conduct espionage and gather insight into their enemy's attacks. Hence, even after persistent attempts, neither side was able to attain a commanding position resulting in a stalemate.

This situation occurred because neither side was able to make substantial progress.

It is always said that the art of defence is as important as the skills required for offence. In such a large-scale battle like this, it was necessary for both sides to prepare their forces and comrades for invasions. In order to break this stalemate, numerous attacks were launched until 1918 but failed because of the strong barrier put up by the opposing side.

INTERESTING FACTS ABOUT TRENCHES:

As the war progressed, the design of the Trenches also improvised. Initially, they started with Trenches just to protect the wounded soldiers but by the later stages, The Allies had developed 4 types of Trenches, each built with a purpose.

Front-Line Trenches**: Also called Firing-and Attack Trenches.** These Trenches weren't built in a straight line but rather changed direction corresponding to natural features such as rivers. This helped the soldiers to defend themselves and gain a good view of their enemies. These trenches were dug in sections because this would prevent the destruction of the entire trench in case of an attack and the damage would only occur in that particular section.

Support Trenches: These were basically as the name suggests trenches that held supplies and men to help the front-line trench soldiers. These were dug behind the front-line trenches.

Reserve Trenches: Basically, these had more supplies and soldiers for support. These were further behind the support trenches.

Communication Trenches: These served as a connection between the other three trenches. Messages, supplies, and men were exchanged in these trenches. The underground paths also connected these trenches with gun shelters and bunkers.

These types of trenches were used by The Allies. The Central Powers had dug their trenches first, (after their defeat in The First Battle of Marne), and hence got the advantage of better soil because they used higher ground. Their trenches were supposedly more well-designed with electricity, beds, and toilets as opposed to The Allies whose trenches were open to the air. In fact, some of the quarters of The Central Powers' trenches were almost 50 ft. below the ground surface!

Having said this, the Trenches definitely were improvised and to a certain extent did provide safety yet the life of soldiers wasn't easy here and they had to face a lot of hardships ranging from basic hygiene to losing their sanity.

Was Trench Warfare Easy?

The answer is a big NO. If there is a gas leakage in your house, doesn't your house stink up? Now imagine the situation in these trenches if there was a gas attack. These trenches were also home to many rats who would eat insects, the remains of humans, and anything else they could find. In fact, these rats consumed so much food that some of them grew up to the size of a cat. These rats kept multiplying and there was absolutely no way to get rid of them.

Interestingly, the soldiers in the trenches believed that the rats would herald an upcoming attack because they would disappear right before an attack.

It wasn't just rats, rather the existence of other creatures such as lice, frogs, and insects also that made life difficult for the soldiers. Men had to shave off their head and body hair to prevent themselves from all sorts of infections. Such factors made the trenches fetid and life in the trenches miserable.

Soldiers even suffered from a situation called "Trench Foot"- at times these trenches got filled with water, toilets overflowed, animals crawled, and the water got infected and soldiers had to be in these for hours continuously. Imagine their plight. Staying in this muddy and infected water gave them Trench Foot which was not only extremely painful but in extreme conditions led to foot amputation.

Source - Hulton Archive/Archive Photos/Getty Images

A picture of the trench warfare that took place during this war

NO MAN'S LAND

This was the name given to the area between two opposing trenches. Usually, this area was about 230 meters but it could go up to 460 meters or come down to 6.4 meters. This area was filled with barbed wire on either side to prevent their opponent from coming close enough to throw grenades into the trenches.

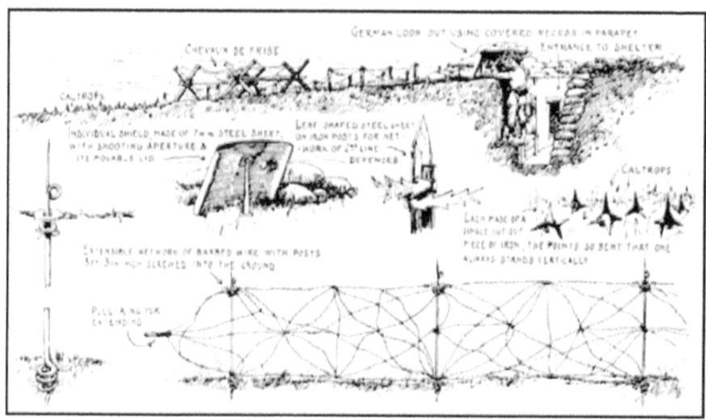

Source - https://spartacus-educational.com/FWWbarbed.htm

This is a drawing of how the Germans placed their barbed wire, made by an Allied spy (spy of The Allies).

Often, paroles were sent out to No-man's land to gain information. These paroles did this at night and had to crawl on their stomachs in order to avoid getting caught and get as close to the opponent's trench as possible. At times, a sentry or guard would be captured and taken back to coerce information out of him. The Germans used a light-shell rocket to kill the soldiers who entered No-man's land. This light-shell rocket was basically an invention where the flare of light hung from a parachute dazzled brightly for a minute and gave the soldiers a chance to kill the opponent. Soldiers often compared this light to being out in the midday sun. A pistol flare was also used by the Germans which only blazed for about 10-15 seconds and was used along with machine gun firing.

RACE TO THE SEA

During this stalemate period, both powers were striving their best to dig tunnels that led all the way to the English Channel. Whichever side's digging skills turned out to be faster and result- bearing would reach the sea first and be able to get around to the other one's side, making it easier to ambush their opponents. But soon, the sides started running out of space and land as more battles took place.

So now, hold your breaths to embark on this blood-shedding and life-threatening journey through the battles that can never be wiped off the face of history. It is important to note that the whole of WWI wasn't one huge battle but rather a chain of a combination of small and big battles that gradually led to its end.

Chapter 08

Countless Battles

From this chapter onwards, we are going to see how the different alliances involved in this war came together to instigate various battles against their rivals and how these shaped the progress of the war.

THE FIRST BATTLE OF YPRES (1914)

This battle, also called The First Battle of Flanders, took place from 19th October to 30th November 1914.

This battle was almost like a subsequent result of the "race to the sea". As the Germans were paving their path through Belgium in this frantic race to reach the sea first, The Allies saw the indispensable need to stop them.

Belgium, France, and Britain together launched an attack on the Germans near a town in Belgium called Ypres in the region of Flanders (specifically West Flanders).

Source - https://www.britannica.com/place/Ypres

A map showing where the town of Ypres was situated

This town of Ypres was considered to be geographically strategic to both sides.

- The Allies did not want the Germans to gain control of this town because it helped block the route of Germans to the French coastal ports.
- This town was also important to the Germans because it was a defensive barrier for their rail network axis in Belgium.

Consequently, the Germans ambushed them on all three sides and the battle went on for some time until it finally descended into Trench Warfare.

While both the Germans (The Central Powers) and the Allies were trying very hard with their mental and physical capacities to outdo each other, this battle was not a clear victory for any.

This wasn't the only battle that took place in the town of Ypres, there were also the succeeding battles: The Second Battle of Ypres and The Third Battle of Ypres, which you will learn about soon.

Some interesting facts:

As rightly said by H.G. WELLS- "If we don't end war, war will end us". Through the journey up till now, you would agree that this statement holds true. But interestingly, like they say that the festival of Christmas brings with it magic, the magic of joy, togetherness, and humanity, and this is exactly what was felt around at that time during this period.

When this war started, many countries joined with the expectation that the war will end by Christmas in December. **'Over by Christmas' was a saying widely used in August 1914.**

We know that the war didn't terminate by Christmas but a lesser-known fact is that from December 24 to 25 (1914), an unpremeditated ceasefire took place on the Western Front referred to as the Christmas Truce. This means that there was almost no fighting for JUST these 2 days. By Christmas Eve, British officers of lower-ranks ordered their troops to not fire or take action until the other side does. This became a policy known as *"Live and Let Live". However, neither this policy nor this truce was authorized by the higher ranked commanders.*

On Christmas, German soldiers came out of their trenches and waved their hands as an indication of **no intent of malice**. British and German soldiers then began to fraternize in No-man's land and also exchanged presents. This truce went on until after New Year's in some areas.

Source - https://www.britannica.com/event/The-Christmas-Truce

An illustration showing British and German soldiers associating during the Christmas Truce, heart-warming right?

Once the Christmas spirit died it seemed its magic also vanished and the soldiers once again refrained from fraternizing with their enemies, mindful of the consequences they would have to face.

It is important to notc that this truce could only happen because of the actions of the junior officers. Thankfully they weren't subjected to any punishment (as this act of humanity wasn't approved by the seniors) because senior commanders were wary of how any court trials or punishments might adversely affect their morale. German soldiers celebrating Christmas

However, any attempts to implement a Christmas truce the following year in 1915 was suppressed and the only ceasefire after this was in 1918 when the *war ended.*

Adolf Hitler, whom I am sure we all are well aware of not just for his cruelty, dictatorship and extreme nationalism, was then just a low-ranking officer. At that time also, he didn't approve of this fraternization and was clearly not going to be a part of it. He didn't even go close to the front trenches (where the celebrations were taking place) rather he condemned those Germans who were associating with their enemies. He reportedly said, "Such a thing should not happen in wartime" and even asked the Germans, "Have you no German sense of honor?

During this battle, Adolf Hitler (who was a German low-ranking officer at that time) won the Iron Cross award. This was the most prestigious award a soldier could be rewarded with for his bravery. Hitler may not seem of much significance right now but as you study the events after World War 1, you will realize the important role he played later on.

Think about how even those 2 days, at that point, with almost no violence & bloodshed must have been such a relief for those soldiers who were otherwise day & night under constant attack.

On the other hand, the fact that Hitler criticized these actions highlights his chauvinism which you should keep in mind when learning about what happened after World War I.

THE BATTLE OF GALLIPOLI (1915-1916)

The Battle of Gallipoli or the Dardanelles Campaign (*February 1915 January 1916*) was a failed attempt by the Allies in 1915 to put an end to the stalemate.

A picture of French troops landing in Lemnos, an area next to Gallipoli, before this battle.

Source - https://thestrategybridge.org/the-bridge/2015/4/24/the-battle-of-gallipoli

This battle of Gallipoli was a land-based element of a strategy intended to allow Allied ships to pass through the Dardanelles (basically a narrow stretch of water connecting to sea or ocean, in this case, the Black Sea), to capture Constantinople (now Istanbul) and knock Ottoman Turkey out of the war.

The Allies thought that invading a different location rather than the one where the Battle of Marne *(France)* had taken place would serve to be in their favor and would pave their way in forcing one of the Central Powers, Turkey out of the war (*Gallipoli is a town in Turkey*).

Source - https://www.britannica.com/event/Naval-Operations-in-the- Dardanelles-Campaign-1915

They wanted to conquer the Gallipoli peninsula (marked in the map above) because if they were successful then they could gain access to the Dardanelles strait which would eventually lead to the Sea of Marmara and then the Black Sea.

Capturing the strait would allow them to enter the Turkish capital of Constantinople, now known as Istanbul, eventually driving Turkey out of the war.

Allied troops at the Gallipoli Peninsula

Source - https://www.britannica.com/topic/Allied-Powers-international-alliance

This army mainly constituted troops from Australia, New Zealand, and France and if they were able to take control of the straits then it would open up a new area with Russia through the Black Sea. This would make communication with Russia easier and provide them with more land for carrying out attacks.

New Zealand and Australia were a part of the British Empire and hence became a part of the war

The Allied forces set in motion attacks on the straits of Dardanelles using their naval forces but, in the process, lost many of their ships.

The time that The Allies used up in reassembling their forces was utilized by the Turks to strengthen their defences. While The Allies managed to set foot on the peninsula, a fierce retaliation from the Turkish army as they made efficient use of their machine guns obstructed their way to the capital and sea.

Trench warfare at the peninsula was also a part of this battle until The Allies decided to evacuate the land thereafter. This proved to be a loss for them as they lost a number of soldiers.

Gallipoli was a costly failure for The Allies: 44,000 soldiers lost their lives on this battlefield.

A picture of Australian troops in a trench

A lighter full of dead or injured troops (A lighter is a kind of boat)

Source - https://thestrategybridge.org/the-bridge/2015/4/24/the-battle-of-gallipoli

THE SECOND BATTLE OF YPRES (1915)

This Battle of 1915 (from 22nd April to 25th May) holds significant value because it involved the use of fatal **chlorine gas.**

The Germans introduced a chlorine gas attack on The Allies hoping it would come as a shock and carve their way to victory. Even though it did come as a shock to The Allies, the immense power and effect of the gas were equally fatal for the Germans as it spread to their trenches as well.

Picture of Australian soldiers wearing gas masks to protect themselves from the gas attack

Source - https://www.britannica.com/event/Second-Battle-of-Ypres

Unfortunately, the Germans were not able to capitalize on the poisonous gas attack because of the unexpected adverse effect it had on them as well.

German soldiers throwing hand grenades while wearing gas masks

Source - https://flashbak.com/behind-enemy-lines-over-100-photographs-of-german-soldiers-fighting-world-war-one-7617/

Meanwhile, Canadian troops (Canada was a part of the British Empire and hence became a part of the war) came up with the brilliant idea of using towels absorbed in urine to prevent themselves from the hazardous effects of this gas. They counter attacked the Germans and hence this war brought no good for the Germans.

A picture of the Germans using chlorine gas

Source - https://www.historycrunch.com/second-battle-of-ypres-in-world-war-i.html#/

Chapter 09

The Battle of Verdun, The Battle of Somme & The Brusilov Offensive

THE BATTLE OF VERDUN (1916)

The Battle of Verdun was a major battle fought in the First WWI between Germany & France. This battle sometimes is also called the "Longest Battle in History" as it lasted from

21st February - 18th December 1916.

Verdun was one of the most ancient cities and fortresses of France. It was of chief importance to the French citizens as it was a symbolic fortress and a national treasure for them. The loss of such a citadel would deal an enormous blow to the French morale.

The Germans wanted to exploit this vulnerability and decided to launch an attack on this city. Not only this, this city of fortresses, Verdun, with its surrounding fortifications along the Meuse River threatened the main German communication lines, which was another important reason for the Germans choice of attack.

fun fact

The attack on Verdun was code-named 'Judgement' by the Germans. It was planned by the German Chief of General Staff named Von Falkenhayn. He said he wanted to "bleed France white" through this attack which meant that he wanted to strip France of all resources.

When this attack started, the number of German troops easily outweighed the number of French troops. Furthermore, the defence at Verdun wasn't very strong from the French army's side which made it easier for Germany to capture the grandest fort protecting Verdun. The French had moved many troops from Verdun to other fronts and even the trenches for defence weren't completely dug up. In this process, the Germans made prudent use of artillery guns and shells to defeat the French soldiers. The Germans anticipated that the French would go to any limits to protect the forts in this city and in the process lose every single army man. This severely alarmed the French and they arranged for more troops to guard the city.

German artillery during this war

Shellfire – attacks using shells

Source - https://time.com/4596494/battle- verdun-photos/

However, the Germans had severely underestimated the French troops and had considered this to be an easy win at the cost of totally neglecting the casualties they would suffer along with the French.

Towards the end of June 1916, The Allies initiated another attack on the Germans which forced the Germans to shift their focus from the battle of Verdun to the *Battle of Somme.*

The Battle of Somme greatly helped the French to save a precious element of their pride, *the city of Verdun.*

Nonetheless, both the French and Germans suffered a colossal number of casualties in this battle of Verdun. In fact, this battle became known as the 'Meat Grinder' because of how deadly it was and the number of fatalities it inflicted.

A picture of Verdun during the war

The battle of Verdun was one of the longest, bloodiest, and most ferocious battles of the war. French causalities amounted to about 400,000 & Germans around 350,000.

Source - https://www.wereldoorlog1418.nl/battleverdun/kortverdun/index.htm

A picture of Germans helping a French wounded soldier – a little bit of humanity amidst the aggressions of this war

THE BATTLE OF SOMME (1916)

The name of this battle originates from the river Somme where it was fought. The horrifying battle of Somme saw more than 1.5 million people deceased or severely hurt or lost and took place between 1st July to 18th November 1916.

> **# fun fact**
>
> The Battle of Somme was initially planned to be an offensive launched in August 1916 and led by the French along with Britain's support. But this didn't go as planned because the Germans attacked the French city of Verdun in February 1916 and the Battle of Somme had to be used to distract the Germans from the city of Verdun.
> Britain shot 1.73 million shells at the Germans in the beginning of this battle.

This battle definitely helped the French save the town of Verdun, their pride but unfortunately, that was just where their victory ended.

This attack only brought causalities and losses for The Allies as the German spies had already warned their troops, giving them a heads up and enough time in advance to prepare for the forthcoming attack.

Britain planned on enforcing a six-day artillery bombardment on the German defences, hoping to demolish them and then ordering their infantry to capture the German lines.

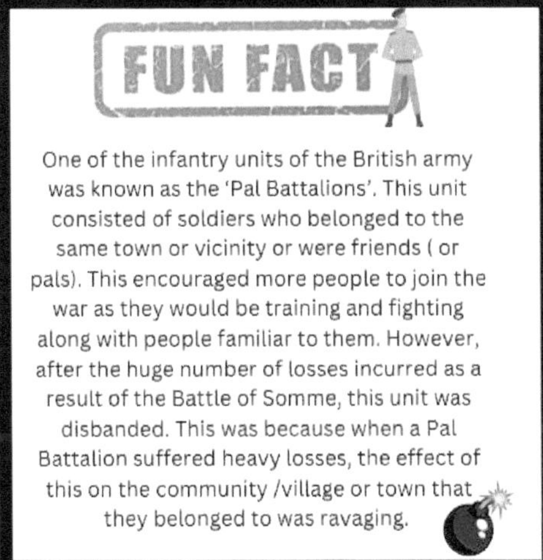
FUN FACT

One of the infantry units of the British army was known as the 'Pal Battalions'. This unit consisted of soldiers who belonged to the same town or vicinity or were friends (or pals). This encouraged more people to join the war as they would be training and fighting along with people familiar to them. However, after the huge number of losses incurred as a result of the Battle of Somme, this unit was disbanded. This was because when a Pal Battalion suffered heavy losses, the effect of this on the community /village or town that they belonged to was ravaging.

In fact, Britain shot 1.73 million shells at the Germans at the beginning of this battle. Little were they aware that the Germans had hidden well inside their shelters and were completely unaffected by this bombardment.

Germans also used barbed wire in front of their trenches for a stronger defence. After the 6-day bombardment, the British soldiers started approaching the German trenches delusional about the fact that they were dead.

The Germans lashed out of their trenches and fired at the soldiers with machine guns. Some of them were trapped in the barbed wire and this battle turned out to be a major loss for The Allies.

This battle was the first ever to make use of tanks, on 15th September. The British launched 48 tanks, like the ones depicted below.

Source -https://www.historyhit.com/facts-about-the-battle-of-the-somme/

Source - https://commons.wikimedia.org/wiki/File:Indian_bicycle_troops_Somme_1916_IWM_Q_3983.jpg

A picture of Indian bicycle troops. India was a British colony at that time

THE BRUSILOV OFFENSIVE (1916)

This offensive, also known as the "June Advance" executed by the Russian troops, took place from 4th June to 10th August (1916), in the eastern front on a part of the region that is now known as Ukraine or namely the towns of Lviv, Kovel, and Lutsk. It was one of the largest assaults afflicted by Russians on Austro-Hungarian forces from which their empire never recovered.

This offensive was the most large-scale and horrifying one effectuated by the Russians, and was targeted basically at Austria-Hungary and resulted in success that served as an astonishment to many.

The credit for this success was solely given to the Russian commander at that time, **General Aleksey Brusilov (picture on the left)**, after whom this offensive has been named.

Brusilov took into account the mistakes his army had committed in the past and ensured they were not repeated. Through this offensive, the Russians emerged victorious against the Austrian-Hungarian troops and afflicted them with huge losses. It was one of the most accurate and well-planned attacks so far from the Russians' side.

 # fun fact

Brusilov kept his plans and preparations for this offensive secretive. The Austrians were greatly taken aback at how judicious the Russians had been about the planning of this attack.

However, as the saying goes, what goes around comes around; the Russians were met with numerous casualties as well, so much so that they weren't able to achieve this great success again in the course of the war.

FUN FACT

This offensive weakened Austria-Hungary so much that it could never play a solid role in the war again. For the rest of the war, Austria-Hungary defended The Central Powers in the trenches against the Italian troops who were even weaker. This left Germany without any substantial support from its ally Austria-Hungary. Isn't this ironic, considering the fact that Germany joined this war because of Austria-Hungary?

Like the Battle of Somme, this attack was also basically put into action to divert the Germans from the Battle of Verdun.

On the first day of the attack, the Russian troops carried out an artillery barrage on the Austrian-Hungarian troops using nearly 2,000 guns. Although the Central Power troops were more in number than the Allied troops, this bombardment and The Central Powers' overconfidence helped The Allies capture 26,000 prisoners in one day alone. The Germans were forced to send troops from Verdun (from the western front to the eastern front) to assist in this battle which resulted in France launching a strong counterattack at Verdun. By the end of this offensive, Austria-Hungary lost 1.5 million men and around 25,000 square kilometres of land.

Although this offensive helped The Allies gain more territory than any other battle, the success of this battle is often overlooked as Russia itself withdrew from the war in 1917 (you will learn more about this in depth later in the book).

 # fun fact

On the first day of this offensive itself, the Russian troops had seized so many Austrian guns that Russian factories had to be converted to make shells for them.

Source -https://schoolshistory.org.uk/topics/world-history/first-world-war/the-brusilov-offensive/

A picture of the Russian cavalry attacking

Chapter 10

Battle at the Sea

WWI was literally a web of battles, starting from the Battle of Ypres, the Battle of Gallipoli, the Second battle of Ypres, and the Battle of Verdun…..Battle of Somme to the Brusilov Offensive, and still many more to come…….The amount of planning that took place and how the battles led to one other… *Crazy, isn't it?*

However, if you have noticed, all these battles up until now were on land, somehow the sea and the navy seemed unaffected. But not for too long because now comes ***"the Battle of Jutland"*, one of the largest sea battles of WWI.**

If you can recollect, a naval army was employed for the Battle of Gallipoli but that was because The Allies wanted to make their way to the peninsula.

Source - https://timemaps.com/history/europe-1914ad/

Britain is an island (as shown on the map) which means that the sea was its only way to obtain all of its supply necessary for the sustenance of its people. Britain had control over the seas and it was essential that they maintain this control if they wanted sustenance. Britain also needed the export and import of goods that was only possible through the sea and we know that Britain had a large empire, right? This means that it needed the sea as its means of communication with its empire, and in no way would Germans overlook this and not attack this crucial part for a win.

But, losing a war at the sea, don't you think would be highly detrimental for the British? Keep reading to learn about the most large-scale naval battle fought in the war – the Battle of Jutland.

THE BATTLE OF JUTLAND (1916)

The Battle of Jutland, fought over two days from 31st May 1916, was the largest sea battle of WWI. It pitted 151 British warships against 99 German ships and was the First and ONLY time two battle fleets confronted each other.

This battle was obviously aimed at the British by the Germans and lasted from 31st May to 1st June 1916.

The Germans knew the salient value that the control of the seas held to Britain and decided to assail their army in a battle at the North Sea.

Winning this battle would give the Germans almost an unbeatable thrust because they could gain control of the sea and hence monitor and probably cut off all British supplies.

However, like Britain, even Germany possessed a few overseas territories, and communication with them wouldn't have been possible without the sea. *For example, it had control of an empire in Africa.*

For the course of this battle, the German commander planned on following an old policy of securing a defensive position while launching attacks on ships along the British Coast.

Both these opponents used their own coded messages to communicate. However, earlier in the war, one of the Allies had sunk a German cruiser in the sea in which they found the body of a German officer holding the German Naval Code Book in his hand, which they took into their custody. This was a major advantage for The Allies as they were able to decrypt all of the Germans' coded messages, without them knowing.

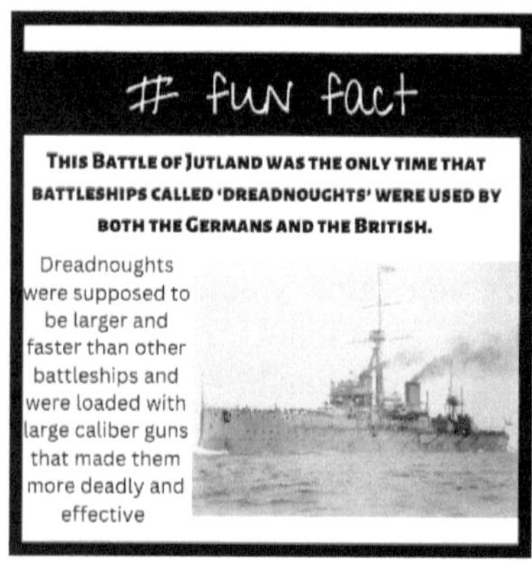

Going back to the attack, the Britishers had already gained an upper hand because they were able to decode all German messages and were well aware of this attack.

Hence, the British put out to sea their entire Royal Navy to oppose the Germans, which took them by shock since they were only expecting a fleet. In the beginning, the Germans seemed to have gained control when they defeated the first two battle cruisers but eventually, the Germans suffered great losses just like Britain.

Source -https://www.britannica.com/event/Battle-of-Jutland

A picture of the ships of the German fleet during this battle

While the British suffered heavier losses than Germany, Germany still decided to withdraw and not launch any more attacks after assessing their losses.

This was considered a British victory, in the sense that they established their naval dominance over other countries.

Chapter 11

Never-ending war field

THE BATTLE OF MESSINES (1917)

Denotes one of the biggest explosions before Atomic Bombs. 19 massive mines beneath German trenches, blasted tons of soil, steel, and bodies into the sky.

Messines was the name of a ridge situated in the south of the city of Ypres and had been under the control of the Germans since 1914.

A picture of the battlefield during this battle

Source - https://sjmc.gov.au/the-battle-of-messines/

 # fun fact

Some military planners had tried to estimate the time it would take for the air to be purged of the debris after the explosion of the mines but their calculation was wrong. The Allied soldiers were covered with smoke and dust when they were preparing to attack, so much so that they could hardly see. However, this had a greater impact on the Germans and this came off as such a shock to them that they could hardly fight or oppose it. Additionally, the terrain was also devastated because of the explosion.

This ridge allowed the German troops a rather powerful position as it looked over Ypres.

This battle from 7th to 14th June 1917 highlighted Britain's desire to annex this ridge which would make launching any attacks in that vicinity easier for them.

This attack was planned scrupulously by a British Officer named General Sir Herbert Plumer. The British troops went through fierce training to ensure a powerful attack. In 1916 itself, the British started laying around 20 mines under the positions of the German troops.

On 7th June at 3:10 am, these mines exploded and became the reason for the deaths and wounding of many German soldiers. Those who weren't physically impaired by this detonation ended up losing their morale. The German casualties were heavy with around 10,000 men killed.

The British were able to attain victory in a week with the help of the well-organized infantry and prudent use of artillery. The British troops were aided by New Zealand, Australian and Canadian troops.

Although this battle was a win for The Allies, it has often been forgotten because it preceded the Third Battle of Ypres which was deadlier.

THE THIRD BATTLE OF YPRES (1917)

Also known as the Battle of Passchendaele (Passchendaele was a Belgium village), this took place in 1917 from 31st July to 10th November in Passchendaele.

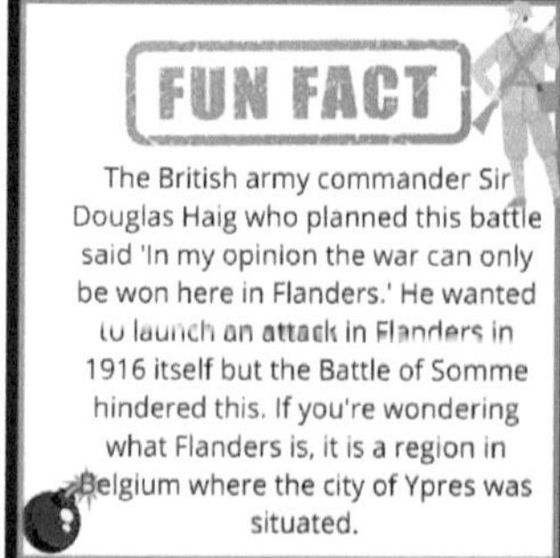

Finally, the Battle of Ypres had come to an end, despite the heavy rains at that time, British and Canadian troops succeeded in taking over the village of Passchendaele.

However, they had captured only about 8 km of land while more than 850,000 soldiers died or were injured.

Source - https://www.iwm.org.uk/history/what-you-need-to-know-about-the-third-battle-of-ypres-passchendaele

A picture showing the results of the rain.

Apparently, men, horses, and war vehicles drowned in mud due to the rains. This weather impaired aerial reconnaissance and the movement of artillery from one place to another also became extremely hard.

During this battle, the Germans implemented an 'elastic defence' (also called 'deep defence' and 'defence in depth') strategy. This meant that instead of secure and heavily guarded trenches at the frontline, a string of defensive zones would be set up with pillboxes and machine-gun posts.

These would weaken the Allied troops as they move past each of these defensive zones.

A picture of a German pillbox

A picture of the entrance to a pillbox

Source- https://ahec.armywarcollege.edu/trail/Pillbox/index.cfm

The Germans planned to launch a strong counter-offensive once the Allied troops were weakened from the Germans' strategy of 'elastic defence'. On the other hand, the British employed a strategy called "bite and hold". The Allies took hold of a small piece of territory which was referred to as "bite" and then held onto it for future use. Another group of troops would pass through these and do the same to another piece of territory.

fun facts

A LITTLE EXTRA INFORMATION ON PILLBOXES

- Pillboxes, also called blockhouses, were very small forts, mostly used by the Germans to strengthen their trench lines. These were concrete constructions with extremely thick walls and the Germans often placed their machine gunners (the army men who operate machine guns) inside these. These thick walls protected the pillboxes from artillery bombardment, but firing was possible through narrow cuts in the wall. During offensives, machine guns were usually placed on top of the pillboxes or at the side of the pillboxes.
- This term pillbox was actually used by the British soldiers because these blockhouses resembled the boxes used by chemists to supply tablets during the war.
- The British did not build many of these pillboxes, their reason being that they "were not worth the cost or the labor". But it is speculated that another reason could be that they were wary that such strong defenses might make the troops more reliant on them and less willing to attack.
- However, it is believed that most army men despised these pillboxes because these made their chances of being killed if captured by their enemies higher than other soldiers.

Source - https://www.bl.uk/collection-items/photograph-of-soldiers-walking-on-duckboard-third-battle-of-ypres

A picture of Australian troops walking on a duckboard track laid due to the muddy ground

Chapter 12

The Allied Blockade

CLARIFICATION CENTER

Since we are looking at the events of this world war in a chronological order, this Allied Blockade should have also been mentioned earlier because it had been in play since 1914. However, it has been brought up only now because it led to events that marked USA's entry into the war.

THE ALLIED BLOCKADE

The Allied Powers, in particular, Britain, showcased their naval dominance by placing a naval blockade on the countries of the central powers right when the war Began in August 1914.

The countries that were subjected to this blockade were Germany, Austria-Hungary, and Turkey.

This curtailed essential food and military supplies from entering The Central Powers.

Britain was able to take under its control and monitor the supplies entering its hostile countries because of the immense naval power it held. It possessed a Royal Navy larger, grander, and more powerful than any other at that time and that shaped the execution of this blockade.

The turmoil escalated in November 1914, when the North Sea was announced as a British 'military area'. This means that this was now an area for the British army. While this violated the rules of international law, most countries did not put across severe opposition. Hence, every merchant ship was rummaged through by the Britishers who inspected for any illegal supplies for Germany.

fun fact

What do you think USA thought of the Allied blockade?
USA, being a neutral country at that time, wanted to continue trading with both sides involved in the war. The blockade meant that they could not successfully trade with The Central Powers which could have an adverse effect on their own economy. Britain did not want to build a hostile relationship with USA but considered the blockade to be too significant to be removed. Luckily for them, they ended up with USA's support in the end.

THE GERMANS COMBAT THE BLOCKADE

In order to outpower the effects of this blockade, in 1915 the Germans deployed submarines, also called U-boats to sink ships in the seas surrounding Britain.

fun fact

WHAT DO YOU THINK THE U IN U Boats stands fOR?

If you're thinking Undersea boats, you're right! In the German language, this was Unterseeboot. These U-boats were way more intricately built than any other submarines at that time and could carry 35 men, travel underwater for 2 hours. Each of these had 12 torpedoes. Torpedoes are underwater missiles that are fired from submarines and attack the target by exploding on reaching it

They aimed at cutting off Britain's supplies, in the hope that they would succumb to The Central Powers as a result of a lack of supplies and food which could lead to major starvation. They did this through the use of **'unrestricted submarine warfare'.**

In this manic run to out beat its opponent, a German submarine sank a British passenger ship called Lusitania in 1915. As a result , a few Americans aboard lost their lives.

This incident provoked the Americans to turn against the Germans.

This sinking was classified as ***'indiscriminate warfare'.***

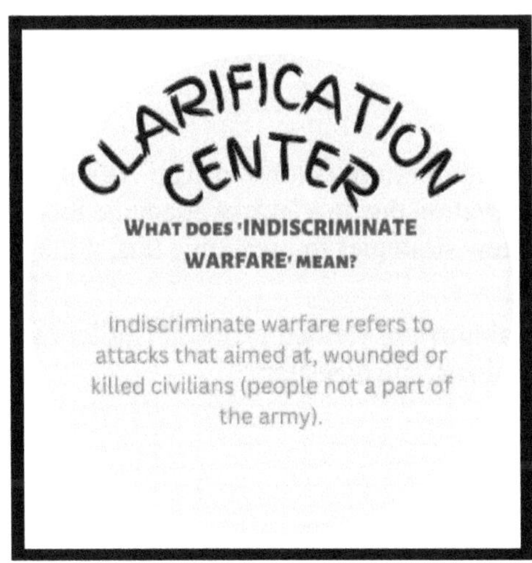

Obviously, as you can imagine, this didn't go down well with USA and Germans internally were wary of the situation.

In their defence, Germans claimed that The Lusitania was carrying ammunition for The Allies.

However, still apprehensive about the notion that the USA might side with The Allies in the war, Germans implemented a temporary policy of abstaining from attacking passenger ships.

Now, it is important to hold onto the word *"temporary"* here as the Germans only temporarily put an end to submarine warfare (due to the reaction of the Americans).

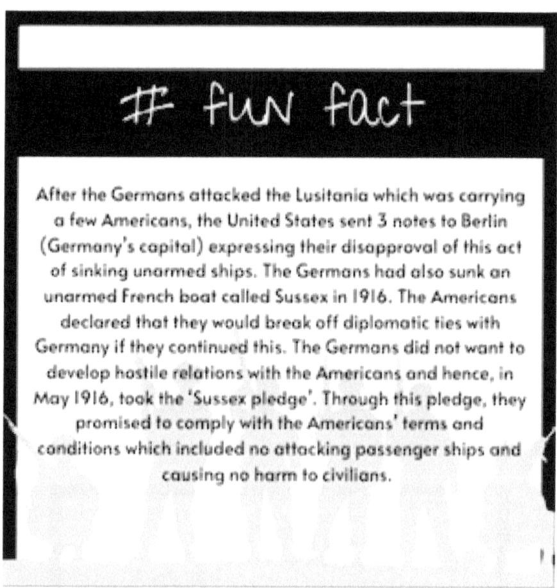

One of the major ramifications of The Allied Blockade for the Germans was starvation due to a lack of adequate food supplies. While they designed a few strategies to overcome this, none of them resulted in great success.

By 1917, malnutrition yielded various disorders and diseases such as scurvy, tuberculosis, and dysentery.

Many of us have experienced the period of the deadly CoronaVirus. The repercussions of this virus have impacted our lives greatly. In 1918, the world was hit by a pandemic called the Influenza virus or the Spanish Flu. We can only imagine the adversities it created amidst the situation of war. Further worsening this situation for The Central Powers was the blockade imposed on them. This is just an example of how life during the war was, full of unyielding hardships.

In 1916, the Germans also issued a policy where it was made mandatory for all men between the age of 17 and 60 to find work, in order to increase the output of goods and services in the country.

If you're on the losing side of a match, then don't you feel this invisible thrust that forces you to do anything possible in your power to somehow win the match? This losing situation in a match is somewhat analogous to the place the Germans held by 1917. With lesser supplies than The Allies, they secured an inferior position.

This insufficient supply of food and military supplies played such a negative role on the Germans that on 31st January 1917, they announced that they would return to the policy of unrestricted submarine warfare. The Germans aimed to destroy ships that were supplying The Allies, hence starving them of food. That sounds scary enough, imagine witnessing or being a part of this!

Remember, this meant that even unarmed passenger ships would be attacked without notice.

Chapter 13

US Enters the War - 1917

Can you imagine the mayhem created after the Germans openly declared that they would resort to their policy of unrestricted submarine warfare? What do you think USA's reaction to this was?

The USA (who was neutral till now) broke all diplomatic relations with Germany on 3rd February (3 days after the Germans' announcement). This indirectly meant that the USA sided with The Allies, but make sure not to say it was one of The Allies yet because it wasn't a part of the war at that particular point in time.

But again, the question arises, why did Germany even resume this policy, knowing that it might earn them a formidable enemy?

This was because the German military leaders devised a plan where they envisaged that their army would emerge victorious in this war much before the US troops could even reach Europe to help The Allies.

Well, now only time can measure the accuracy of their prediction!

A few hours after the US terminated diplomatic relations with Germany, an American liner "Housatonic" was attacked by a German U-boat. Towards late February, US had already started preparing their troops for war while Germans U-boats continued sinking American ships throughout February and March, causing deaths of several Americans.

Finally, the USA's entry into the war was marked when they declared war on Germany on April 4, 1917. Austria-Hungary was also later subjected to a declaration of war by the US in December 1917.

ANOTHER REASON FOR U.S.A.'S ENTRY

Way before World War 1, from 1846 to 1848, America and Mexico went to war over some land which resulted in Mexico having to cede this territory to America. This territory is actually Texas in present day America! The Germans tried to use this to their advantage and sent Mexico a telegram, referred to as the "Zimmermann Telegram", offering them a deal. The deal stated that if Mexico sided with Germany during this war, the Germans would help them reconquer this territory which they had lost to the Americans. However, in January 1917, Britain intercepted this telegram and decoded it using the German naval code book which they had laid their hands on earlier. Britain then informed USA about it and this became another reason why USA declared war on Germany. This was because the telegram implied that Germany would invade USA in order to help Mexico regain Texas. Once USA became aware of this, its press spread the story the following week. After this telegram went viral, Mexico chose to remain neutral. Despite Germany's rather desperate attempt at obtaining more support, The Allies managed to gain the upper hand.

How did Britain react to Germany's policy of unrestricted submarine warfare?

By 1917, Britain adopted a convoy system where all merchant ships travelled in large groups called convoys. This was done as a defensive measure against Germany's policy of unrestricted submarine warfare. These ships were shielded from attacks as they were protected by the British royal navy, which obliterated the German U-boats.

Chapter 14

An Insight Into Russia The Russian Revolution

As we have studied earlier, the Brusilov Offensive of 1916 greatly weakened Russia in terms of its economy and military forces, so much so that the Russians were not able to repeat this success in WWI. Large scale battles like these have devastating outcomes. The effect of this was heightened in Russia because it was already poor and destitute, and soon the consequences were too costly to be handled. Russia's economy was neither fully developed nor was it self-sufficient. This resulted, in a major crisis and upheaval and even the ruler, Tsar Nicholas II could not bring the situation under control.

He was an autocratic leader, which means that he exercised his power excessively and all decisions were made by him, with little or no advice from others. Tyrant and oppressive, many people were against this type of governance (autocracy). Along with the predicament of poverty, many Russian soldiers weren't heavily equipped and were poorly guided.

Nicholas (the ruler at that time) thought he could enhance the performance of the Russian soldiers fighting WWI by going to the battlefield himself to lead them.

fun fact

It is believed that Rasputin (the queen's advisor) could not be murdered. In 1914, Rasputin recuperated after being stabbed in the stomach even after losing a lot of blood. In 1916, the nobles who killed Rasputin first poisoned him and then bombarded him with bullets. He still seemed to be alive after this. They then threw him into an ice-cold river. According to autopsy reports, the poison did no harm to him and no trace of it was found in his body. They thought he died because of a bullet fired at his head. Interesting, right?

In his absence, his wife fulfilled his duties as the king. She paid heed to the advice provided by a man called Grigori Rasputin (a mystic and self-proclaimed holy man) who supposedly possessed healing powers. These powers are what helped him gain her favor but the advice he gave her worsened the situation in the country.

As a result, Rasputin was assassinated by members (in 1916) of the Russian nobility (aristocrats) who opposed the advice he gave to Alexandra.

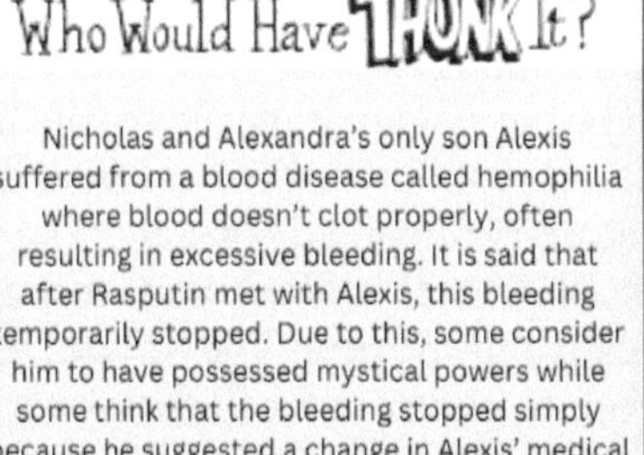

Petrograd, the capital of Russia, (now known as Saint Petersburg), witnessed a protest due to severe food shortages and scarcity of fuel which was a necessity for winters. These protests began on 8th March 1917 and went on for 8 days. The condition was so dire that the soldiers who were tasked to quell the protest ended up joining it. As a result of this anarchy, around 1300 people were either killed or injured. By the time Nicholas returned from the battlefield, he was informed that he had lost the army's support. This meant that his rule had no power, leading him to abdicate his throne.

The February Revolution & The October Revolution

WHAT DOES 'REVOLUTION' MEAN?

Revolution is a forcible overthrow of a government or social order, in favor of a new system.

Meanwhile, an interim government was set up, which was a committee of 12 people who aimed at accomplishing the tasks of the government.

These 12 men gave themselves a name – The Provisional Government. This became known as *The February Revolution* because it took place in that month. However, these men were unable to handle the crisis that well. The biggest hindrance lay in the fact that they wanted to win the war instead of withdrawing Russia from it. Being a part of the war meant that the scarcity remained constant. The government started facing opposition from several soldiers and workers who soon set up their own councils called the *Soviets.* The Soviets led by people known as the Bolsheviks rose to power and had their own army consisting of soldiers that they called the *Red Guards.* Eventually, they seized all power from the Provisional Government.

The Bolsheviks made the civilians content in many ways. The slogan used by their leader Vladimir Lenin was *"Peace, bread, and land".* Given the war situation, the Russians were devoid of even basic needs and wanted sufficient food and a place to live. Lenin's slogan promised to provide the Russians with peace, food, and a place to live in, increasing the support for the Bolsheviks. This was the second revolution and known as the *October Revolution.*

Another important fact is the Bolshevik's immense belief in a type of government called the communist government. While you don't necessarily have to acquaint yourself with the term communism right now, communism is an ideology where there is no private property and everything is owned by the government and then distributed. This was invented by a philosopher called Karl Marx.

Now, what do you think was the Bolsheviks' first step after they rose to power? If you're thinking that it was withdrawing Russia from the war, you're absolutely correct.

In March 1918, Lenin signed a peace treaty with The Central Powers. A peace treaty can be described as a formal agreement ending a state of war between 2 or more countries. This particular treaty between Russia and The Central Powers was called the Brest-Litovsk Treaty. On one hand, this treaty demanded a lot of Russian property and land but on the other, it was a sigh of relief for those who wanted Russian involvement in the war to come to an end.

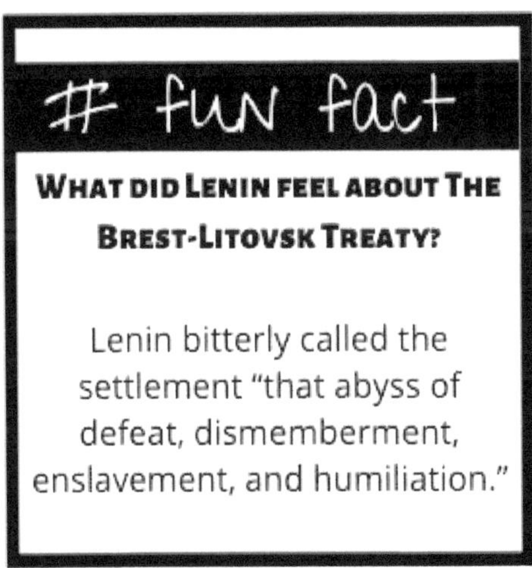

Before we proceed any further, let's analyze the situation of the rivals during this time, in 1918.

Chapter 15

The Central Powers VS The Allies

Strengths of The Central Powers

By 1918, The Central powers had anchored a rather powerful position in the war. After Russia conceded, numerous troops could be repositioned to other war fronts; it basically meant a rival down for them. In addition, Romania was propelled to surrender to Germany after it captured its capital and invaded most of the country. The causalities in Italy were way too high and disastrous hence The Central Powers did not have to fear major opposition from their end. In addition, to the further dismay of The Allies, France experienced mutiny from army corporals due to the extreme success of German defences. Mutiny meant that the army corporals defied orders from their seniors because they realized that any offence at the time was tantamount to walking into death. Not surprisingly, it did take a while for France to get its army back on its feet.

Strengths of The Allies

However, as it is widely said, excess of anything upsets the balance of the world, The Allies did have some aces up their sleeves. For starters, the naval blockade they imposed on The Central Powers showed its wonders and since Germany's counter offensive to that (the unrestricted submarine warfare) failed, starvation flooded these countries and inevitably caused diseases and deaths. Now, remember we talked about France and Britain owning huge empires? So, don't you think that at such a crucial time, they would put all their resources to use? Hence, Britain and France called upon their empires. For example, countries like Canada, Australia, and New Zealand were all linked to the British Empire. Another instance of this is that Chinese men worked in France as laborers to compensate for the lack of labor due to the repercussions of the war. India also stepped in with its extraordinary military power, supporting The Allies in a full-fledged manner. Furthermore, they did manage to sustain their control of the sea and were exceeding in aircraft models and other weapons such as poison gas. Their supply of resources had not been cut off like The Central Powers' and they could always turn to their empires for any help, which included resources. It is also believed that the leaders of The Allies were able to instil a vehement feeling of nationalism and resilience in the civilians, provoking them to combat any attack more effectively than other countries. On the contrary, this wasn't the same for the Germans. It is believed that the leader of Germany, Kaiser Wilhelm II, did not make public speeches at all and his advisors were always skeptical about what he would say. This meant that the Allied soldiers were better motivated and assured.

Further, the U.S.A joined the war a month after Russia left. It almost seems as if even though The Allies lost a country, they gained the support of a stronger, more powerful, and more promising country.

Chapter 16

The Beginning of the End

By now I am sure you would have had an overview of how the war proceeded. The strategies, the plans, the innumerous battles fought and the loss of lives were unaccountable yet the desire and greed in the name of pride and honor were intact. Both The Allies & Central Powers had strengthened and weakened yet the urge to win was growing stronger. Some countries like Russia had laid their guns down yet others like the USA had joined hands with The Allies. On the other hand, Germany was not easily going to surrender rather they wanted to win at any cost.

We have now come to the last stretch of the war so let's see how things shape up from here....

In 1918, the then German General, Erich Ludendorff was intent on approaching the final battle by hook or by crook. In this irresistible urge, driven by the adverse effects of the blockade on The Central Powers, he planned an Offensive that became known as the Ludendorff Offensive or the Spring Offensive. Ludendorff wanted to deploy all the soldiers, including those that were now free from Russian territories into action in **ONE ALL OUT FINAL OFFENSIVE**, hoping to attain victory.

THE LUDENDORFF OFFENSIVE (1918)

This lasted from March 1918 to July 1918, designed by the German General Erich Ludendorff.

Throughout this offensive, the Germans availed the most rigorously trained men of their army called the *Stormtroopers*. If they wanted to go all out, they had to do it with the best of their forces. These men had been trained differently and equipped with more powerful weaponry. These men disrupted communication & supply lines and ambushed the enemy from the back.

In addition, the Germans also made use of their new A7V tanks, an advanced form of weaponry for greater destruction.

Bergmann submachine gun used by Stormtroopers

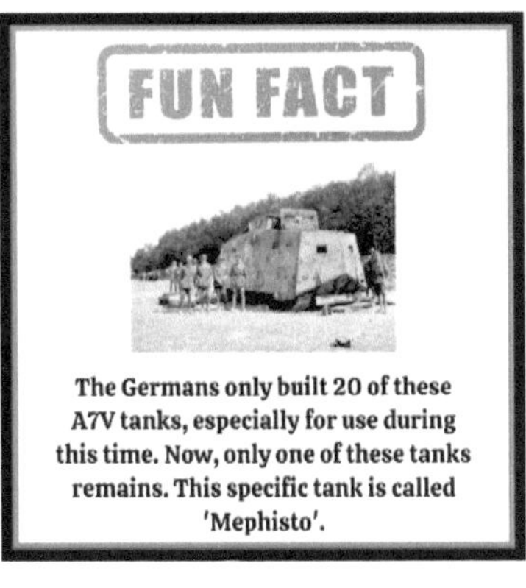

The Stormtroopers made use of newly made weapons like this *'Bergmann submachine gun'* immensely during this offensive. *These were also helpful during trench warfare.*

However, the Germans were overly reliant on their Stormtroopers. Due to food shortage, these soldiers were literally starved, as a result, they halted at various stops to plunder food.

Although they possessed technologically advanced vehicles such as tanks and planes, they were running short on fuel due to the blockade. It is said that the Germans were forced to put a halt to their offensive ample times because of the shortage of supplies.

Chapter 17

The Beginning of The Ludendorff Offensive

On March 21, 1918, Erich Ludendorff initiated The Ludendorff Offensive or The Spring Offensive with their first attack known as Operation Michael, which was actually the code name for this attack.

OPERATION MICHAEL

The main aim of "Operation Michael" was to attack at such a point on the Western Front that in the process of defending themselves, the French and British armies would split.

On 21st March 1918, the Germans commenced this attack with a heavy bombardment at 4:40 am in the morning. This artillery barrage is considered to be one of the most powerful ones in the war. What worked advantageously for the Germans was that while the British were expecting an attack over a vast area of land, the Germans chose to penetrate and attack a concentrated area.

The British were left flummoxed and forced to retreat. It is believed that during this attack, the Germans managed to recapture all the land that they had lost around the River Somme in the last two years in just 5 days.

Soon, the Germans approached the French town of Amiens. This town was of utmost importance to The Allied powers as it was a

significant railway junction and without it, the Allied countries would have found it extremely difficult to transport supplies and troops to the front battle line.

The situation seemed dire for The Allies but they were saved by a bristle when the Australian forces were called in on 25th March to recede Germany's progress.

Even though this offensive didn't furnish the results the Germans were hoping for, their persistence didn't alter. **Their next battle was called the Second Battle of Marne.**

THE SECOND BATTLE OF MARNE (1918)

But why is it called the SECOND Battle of Marne?

Dig deeper into your brain, you know this! It's because the first battle of Marne had already taken place earlier in 1914. This battle lasted from 15th July to 6th August 1918 and Ludendorff chose to call this the *"peace offensive"* because he thought that emerging victorious from this would finally bring peace for the Germans.

American soldiers had also started arriving in France. It is said that when they first arrived in France, many doubted if they would be able to stand up to the German soldiers who had been involved in this bloody battle since 1914.

According to reports, many American soldiers arrived for this war without even a weapon in their hands.

However, it is important to note that the Germans had lost many of their army men and were constantly haunted by the lingering hunger and shortage of supplies. Apparently, a German prisoner held in the force of The Allies had been coerced to let out information on where and when the Germans' next assault would be. This was definitely a major disadvantage for the Germans as The Allies knew their next move.

The Germans initiated this attack with a barrage or bombardment of the enemies' trenches. But here comes the twist, they bombarded what they thought were the enemies' trenches. The French had lined up some misleading trenches which the Germans perceived to be the real ones. The actual trenches were barely affected by the bombardment. How smart and shrewd, right? This was thought of by the French commander-in-chief and it did yield positive results for them.

Now, as the Germans advanced after this redundant barrage, they were ambushed by The Allies who then assailed the Germans.

The Germans were taken aback as The Allies set in motion their counter offensive and managed to capture many German soldiers and their weapons. The losses of this battle were so mammoth that the Germans called off their Spring Offensive.

U.S.A.'s enormous support *(to The Allies)* in this battle helped define it as a paramount military power.

Another cardinal factor to note is the fact that this Second Battle of Marne was the last and the ultimate effort by the Germans to win the war, meaning that this was the last substantial offensive they launched.

Along with help from Australian, Canadian and American troops, Britain and France's counter offensive battle had clearly triumphed.

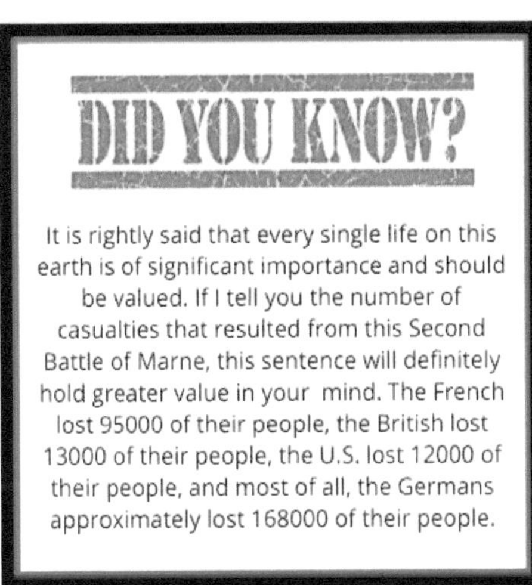

What do you think would have happened if the Spring Offensive paid off and the Germans won the Second Battle of Marne? Our history and perhaps the present would be different in ways we can't even imagine!

It is said that just during the Spring Offensive, the German army suffered as many as a million losses. It's almost as if all hope for victory had been drained out of the Germans. Even though The Allies experienced huge losses as well, remember they had the tremendous support of the Americans, be it in terms of troops, weaponry, or other supplies.

This battle was definitely the last one initiated by The ***Central Powers*** but definitely not the one that ended the war. It was The ***Allies' offensive*** that we could call the last and deciding battle.

This was the ***Battle of Amiens!*** *(named after the French town, Amiens)*

Chapter 18

The End of the End

THE BATTLE OF AMIENS (1918)

This was an Allied initiative that took place from 8th August to 11th August 1918 after their victory in the Second Battle of Marne.

This attack included an estimated number of 75,000 men, 500 + tanks, and 2,000 planes that all constituted to its favorable outcome.

The Allies now wanted to literally shove the Germans out of France and they decided to carry out this attack at Amiens. This battle of Amiens was the first among a series of battles launched by The Allies conjointly called the Hundred Days.

This Hundred Days campaign lasted from 8th August till 11th November or essentially till the end of this horrific, dreadful & frightful war.

This attack was a clear Allied success with them seizing numerous German troops and weapons.

Source - https://collection.nam.ac.uk/detail.php?acc=1972-08-67-2-185

A picture of the captured German prisoners in November 1918 from one of the last attacks of the 'Hundred Days Offensive'

All this prompted General Erich Ludendorff (the German General) to label 8th of August as the *"Black day"* of the German army because this had exterminated all their motivation and confidence.

The British army had captured approximately 13,000 people and more than 300 guns. In a war scenario, the presence or absence of even one gun can make a difference, so imagine what taking away of more than 300 guns must have been like for Germany.

On 8th August itself, the Germans suffered somewhere around 30,000 losses while in comparison, The Allies only suffered 6,500 losses.

An illustration of ground attack aircraft like this Bristol fighter which played an important role in the advances of August 1918.

Source - https://ww1.nam.ac.uk/stories/lieutenant-richard-talbot-kelly/#.Y2IN9-xBy3I

German prisoners captured and escorted by the Canadian troops in a communication trench during August 1918

Source - https://ww1.nam.ac.uk/stories/ captain-daniel-hickey/#.Y2IN2exBy3J

IMPORTANT FACTS:

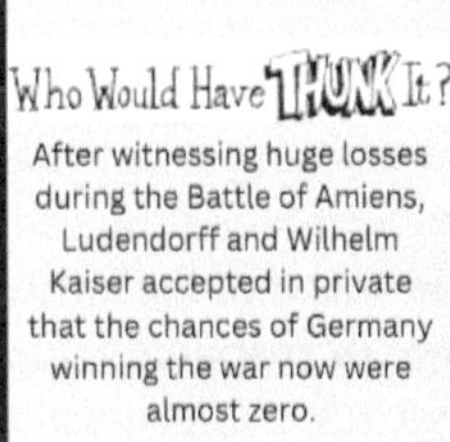

- The Battle of Megiddo, which took place from 19th to 25th September 1918, was an offensive led by the British on the Ottoman Empire. This battle, along with a few successive ones, resulted in the Ottoman Empire withdrawing from the war on 30th October and an armistice was signed. An armistice is an official agreement to put an end to a state of war between countries. The name of this battle comes from the place it was fought in: Megiddo, in Palestine
- On September 24th, 1918, Bulgaria sought an armistice from The Allies. This was in play five days later and Bulgaria exited the war on 29th September. By 1918, the Germans were forced to move their troops who were assisting the Bulgarian troops to the western front where more deadly battles were taking place. The Allies exploited this and launched an attack on Bulgaria (The Vardar Offensive, from 15th September to 29th September). The Bulgarian army was routed which gave way to mutiny (refusal to obey orders from people of authority). Bulgaria had no choice but to surrender.
- On November 3rd, 1918, Austria-Hungary surrendered to The Allies. This was mainly because by 1918, its troops were so exhausted and its economy was so damaged that withdrawing from the war seemed like the only option. An armistice was signed on November 3rd (effective from November 4th) and this marked the end of Austria-Hungary's participation in the war.
- *Let's now have a look at how well the Germans were holding up in 1918.*

Chapter 19

The Moment of Truth

Germany in 1918

I am sure by now you would have realized how the Allied Blockade had dented Germany in more than one way. It won't be wrong to say that one of the biggest and most crucial reasons for the Germans downfall was - the Allied blockade. The result of this blockade was that the entire country was swept by extreme hunger and a shortage of resources. For example, the shortage of coal made extreme cold weather unbearable. Basic necessities like soap and washing powder were also running short. In such conditions, diseases and viral cases of flu inevitably tend to take over and the Germans found themselves facing this same predicament.

Improving or degrading the country's situation was in the ruler: *Kaiser Wilhelm's* hands but he did not take appropriate action. Maybe by trying to make peace with The Allies, he would have mitigated the situation. His failure to act astutely turned minds against him.

Germany also faced a situation of mutiny during this period. The German naval command wanted to set in motion one last attack against the British in the North Sea in October 1918. Despite being given the order 5 times, the sailors of the battleships refused the order to put to sea for battle. These sailors were arrested but this resistance pervaded throughout Germany. Sailors began heavily protesting against this, conducted mass meetings, and were soon joined by soldiers and workers. These sailors, soldiers, and workers then established councils to manage the towns, and these councils were headed by socialists.

But what is socialism? Socialism is a type of government where property is owned publicly rather than privately. Now if memory serves you all right, a while ago we learned about communism, the definition of which seemed pretty similar right? So, are they the same thing?

#fun fact

Communism was discovered by a man called Karl Max. He used the basis of socialism to come up with this form of living. If you want to expand your knowledge on this , you can refer to the book 'Communist Manifesto', written by Karl Max and a German socialist and philosopher named Friedrich Engels.

Well, not exactly. Though both socialism and communism aim at lessening the disparity between the poor and the rich by distributing property and resources more equally and fairly, there are some minor differences between them. While socialism allows more freedom and can be followed in a democracy, communism is said to allow lesser freedom and is usually not followed in a democracy.

Coming back to Germany's situation at hand, after these councils were established, the ruler Kaiser Wilhelm renounced his throne on 9th November 1918. The army informed him that they would no longer back him up after which he left Germany and went to settle in the Netherlands, a country that was neutral in the war.

Kaiser Wilhelm was replaced by Friedrich Ebert who led the biggest and most influential socialist party in Germany.

What do you think Friedrich Ebert did as soon as he came into power? What would your guess be?

On 11th November 1918, he surrendered to The Allies, bringing an end to this war. Yes, Germany surrendered! While many Germans strongly opposed this and believed that if Germany had continued fighting, it would have won the war, the decision to surrender felt sensible at the time. The war kept deteriorating the situation in Germany and their recent losses had demotivated them further.

An armistice was signed between The Central Powers and The Allies at 5 am in the morning in a railroad carriage in France on 11th November 1918. An armistice is like a documented ceasefire, if that makes it simpler for you to understand. This armistice became valid from 11 am that day and officially ended this terrific war.

The leaders who signed this armistice were called the 'November criminals' by many who believed that Germany would have won the war if it continued fighting. They believed that they had been stabbed in the back by those who surrendered. This is often referred to as the

'Stab in the back' myth which is a belief that the Germans did not lose the war on the battlefield, but were betrayed by the leaders and politicians who signed the armistice.

fun fact

The words of an Allied officer on November 11, 1918: "Entering a village as we follow behind the Brigade, our drums struck up the "Marseillaise". The populace became wildly excited, not having heard their National Anthem for a long time. An old man wearing an old fashioned night cap opened a window and leaned so far forward, cheering and waving his arms that one feared he might topple out," The "Marseillaise" is the national anthem of France. These words should give you an idea of how victory felt like and how joyously it was celebrated!

Contribution of women towards the war

This book would be incomplete without talking about the contribution of women to this war.

At the time of this war, women were not allowed to vote or serve in the military in most places. However, during the war, many women replaced the working men who had been sent to the battlefields to keep the production in the industries going. This was because many men were often 'conscripted' or 'drafted' into the army, which means that it was mandatory for them to be a part of the military (usually for a set period of time).

During the war, women in Russia, Serbia, and Germany often fought in battles (although this wasn't that common). However, this was not allowed in countries such as Britain and France. Hence, women often disguised themselves to be able to partake in the war but were usually dismissed when discovered. Many women also worked to support the military as nurses, doctors, ambulance drivers, and translators. In many countries, women did become heroes and were recognized with medals awarded by their own countries and other countries.

This World War, from 1914 to 1918, persisted for approximately 1564 days. Not only was this a long and excruciating period but the number of causalities that took place throughout the duration of this war far exceed the length of it. Apart from the causalities that occurred, the physical and mental distress that this war inflicted on each and every citizen of the countries involved is just beyond imagination.

This World War changed the dynamics of the entire world in ways that no other war had been able to earlier. These countries put a halt to their violent acts of aggression but do you think peace and stability were restored in the world after this?

11 November definitely marked the end of World War 1 but was this the end of all world wars?

Lastly, a little tribute to the fallen, but not forgotten

For those who wiped their fears and walked straight into hell
For those who embraced this bloodshed with courage & mighty strength
For those who led their countries with hearts so full of pride
For those who grieved inside yet gave their families love & strength
For those who may have gone, but can never be forgotten
For those are the ones who gave us our lives, at the cost of theirs

For the fallen, but not forgotten

www.ingramcontent.com/pod-product-compliance
Ingram Content Group UK Ltd.
Pitfield, Milton Keynes, MK11 3LW, UK
UKHW040031200726
13854UKWH00001B/467